# Planting Wild Grapes

## A Collection of Poems
### by
### Kathleen Kramer

For Jack

And for our Dear Ones

ISBN 978-0-9837768-8-8

Books are available through the publisher and at www.amazon.com, as well as at bookstores in the Ithaca, NY area.

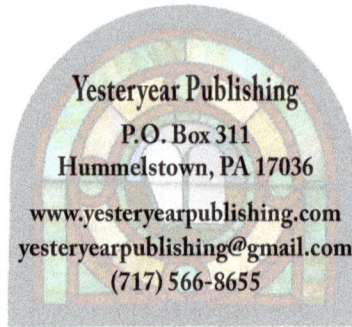

**Yesteryear Publishing**
P.O. Box 311
Hummelstown, PA 17036

www.yesteryearpublishing.com
yesteryearpublishing@gmail.com
(717) 566-8655

**Photo credits:**

French acrobat Philippe Petit balances on a tightrope strung between the World Trade Center's Twin Towers in 1974, cover of *Man on Wire*. Reprinted by permission of Skyhorse Publishing, Inc.

WALKING MAN I, sculpture by Alberto Giacometti, courtesy of the Herbert F. Johnson Museum of Art at Cornell University, Ithaca, NY. (Photo by Kathleen Kramer.)

WEATHERSIDE, 1965 tempera on panel © Andrew Wyeth. Collection of Ann and Jim Goodnight, promised gift to the North Carolina Museum of Art, Raleigh.

FROSTBITTEN, 1962 watercolor on paper © Andrew Wyeth, Private Collection.

EVENING VELVET, 2007 acrylic on canvas © Anita Dore, Collection of Anita and Sal Strods, Skaneateles, New York.

## ACKNOWLEDGEMENTS ~

The author gratefully acknowledges the publications in which the following poems have appeared:

"Currency" – *The Comstock Review*

"Planning the Family Reunion," "The Seasons of Trees," "Utah, off State Route 24" – *Avocet, a Journal of Nature Poems*

"Not Going to Buttonwood," "Still," "Their Stone," "Visiting Hours" – *The Healing Muse*

In addition, "Churchyard" was previously published in *Boiled Potato Blues*, a collection of poems by the author. "Then… and Then" was previously published in *Inside the Stone*, a chapbook by the author.

Deep appreciation to my poetry group, The High Noon Poets, for their expert and sensitive critiques of nearly every poem in this collection. Warm thanks, also, to Jack Hopper for his encouragement and advice; to Barbara Warland for her careful reading of the manuscript and her insightful comments on its organization; to Nan Edmunds for facilitating the publication of this collection and for her creative talents in layout and design. And, of course, to my husband, Jack, for his unfailing interest and for championing my work when I doubted its worth: Thank you for 45 years of encouragement!

Cover and book design by E. Nan Edmunds.

Cover photograph by Green Deane, Naturalist, Forager, Educator and Author. Visit EatTheWeeds.com.

Author photograph by Jack Kramer.

# ABOUT THE AUTHOR ~

Growing up in Pennsylvania's coal mining and farming region, Kathleen Kramer's early life was influenced by the solidity of the earth and the rhythm of seasons.

At 19, she left for the city and spent five years working in Washington, DC for the Department of Defense. There followed a stint in Maine where subsistence farming took her back to the land. A second marriage brought her to Long Island, where she and her husband Jack reared their three sons in Northport, a small town on Long Island Sound. During that time and over a period of 10 years of balancing classes, family and work, Kathy earned a BA at Empire State College and an MLS at C.W. Post.

Now, following retirement from the Boyce Thompson Institute at Cornell, Kathy lives with her husband in New York's Finger Lakes area where she writes poetry and plays. Again, the natural world and changing seasons have assumed center stage. It's these foundational elements and the strength of generational ties which largely inform Kathy's poems.

## AUTHOR'S NOTE ~

*Planting Wild Grapes* – The title of this book was given to me in a vivid dream. It lived in my mind and heart for several years as I pondered its meaning. Why plant wild grapes? Why do something so clearly unnecessary? Something that will, if unhindered, take care of itself?

So far, the closest I have come to the truth it may hold is that we are called to participate in our lives and in the life of the world. To be deeply engaged—to love, to honor everything, even our pain. To taste, to savor it all. Hold it close, then when the time comes, with grace and thanksgiving, to let it go.

Writing these poems has been one of the ways I've found to love this "one wild and precious life." *

KK

* From "A Summer Day," by Mary Oliver

# FOREWORD ~

In *Planting Wild Grapes* Kathleen Kramer circumnavigates her adult life, debarking from her rural Pennsylvania home-ground to "The Clarity of Crossroads," the section that describes her leaving home and her struggles in Maine on a subsistence farm with her first husband, whom she leaves for a happier marriage, but not without inner scars. In the next section—"Yesterday's Snow, Tomorrow's Garden,"—spring's hope emerges, along with more children and grandchildren, the pleasures of nature, art, and her new marriage, poignantly summed in poems of advancing years like "The Oldest People at the Party." This section closes with works that speak of letting go of life as a parent of young people. The book's last section, "Winter Trees Have No Secrets," brings us full circle, in which the poet writes of aging and loss, but not without ironic admixtures of joy and humor, as the book's very title—*Planting Wild Grapes*—playfully suggests.

Kramer's new collection is the successor but not displacer of her earlier *Boiled Potato Blues*. Present again in this new work is her transformative ability to endure the pain of life, and her reverence for but not subservience to that life. Her word-web lures us to earlier times of 5- and 10-cent stores, porch swings, and Dinty Moore Stew. Her craft imposes on us a saner pace than our twenty-first-century bustle and breathlessness, and teaches us to observe, not just see, the pleasures of life. Her written world is one of toughness, moral authority, and best of all, lucky readers, consummate poetic sense.

—Jack Hopper, Poet Laureate of Tompkins County, NY

# CONTENTS ~

Part Three – Yesterday's Snow, Tomorrow's Garden               49

# Planting Wild Grapes

Every day at dawn I go down to the river,
fill my bucket to the brim and wash stones.
Big or small, I take all that come to hand,
dip them in my pail, rub them between my palms
and drop them back into the river. I listen
for the satisfying sound—the watery thunk—
as they settle among their fellows.

At mid-day I wade the waves of goldenrod
to the center of the sunny field behind the barn.
Beneath my feet, my shadow crouches,
small and black. The candle in my hand
stands tall, like me, its wick waiting for
the match, prepared to be proud of a flame
invisible in the noonday light.

Sunset finds me again at river's edge, a teacup
cradled in my hands. It holds rainwater caught
in the downpour at dinnertime. I lift it up
to the sinking sun, see the rim turn gold,
then tip the cup, spilling rain into the river.
Tomorrow, if I keep to my course,
there will be time to plant wild grapes.

Deepening, almost still . . .

# Her Face

*For our mother*

I'd forgotten rivers don't freeze smooth
From childhood I remembered the Susquehanna
just above the dam where the water was held back

    deepening     almost still
      and the ice
   like a sheet of polished steel
   stretched   from shore to shore

But   unconstrained   it runs over rocks
takes its chances with boulders and fallen logs
splashes up to bite the wind

               freezes into a landscape
    of peaks and ridges
         crevasses and crags
   a portrait of obstacles   overcome

# Relatively Small and Not Very Conspicuously Marked

*...of the Song Sparrow,*
*Smithsonian Bulletin 237*

This porch is the perfect place
for an old man.  And for me,
sitting beside him on the rusty glider.

This porch railing is the perfect place
for the few seeds he's sprinkled there
so we can watch the song sparrow

feed her fledgling—bigger now
and more robust than she—
his last meal of the day.

A voice calls: *Brian, Briii-an.*
This neighborhood has changed since
I moved away, but the old man knows.

*That's Lorraine,* he says.  From somewhere,
the smell of hamburgers and onions frying.
Evening flows under the trees, claims

the grassy lawn blade by blade.
Rain begins to fall with a sound like sighing.
I didn't know fireflies flew in the rain.

# Ode to the 5 & 10

O, Marketplace of Childhood!
O, Bazaar of Youth Long Spent!
Purveyor of geegaws and gimcracks,
of celluloid dolls with stiff legs
and bright-cheeked faces,
of chocolate drops behind glass cases
doled out in tiny white bags.

Our only source for Christmas gifting—
*Evening in Paris,* bottles cobalt
blue. *Old Spice* in white, the ship
on its side sailing forever the same
two waves. Box of chocolate
covered cherries for Grandma,
who will give us more than half.

And the tools for budding seduction—
*Tangee* lipstick, pale in the tube to placate
our mothers, block of mascara in a little
red box, polish for nails still stubby,
bras lined up, cups pointing skyward—
miniature mountain ranges of white,
the perky promise of circular stitching.

O, to wander again your maze
of aisles, smell your old wood floors,
oil spread to damp the dust, feel
nickels knotted in the corner of a hanky,
face again the delicious decision of what
to buy, the sweet anguish of bubble pipe
or barrette, comic book or compact.

19

# Rhododendrons

A hometown is where rhododendrons rest
their arms on porch railings, cover
front room windows with leafy fingers,
leathery and green. It's where you can still
pay your water bill at a counter in the back
of the drug store and where the radio station
broadcasts obituaries at noon on Fridays.

It's where, after 60 years away, you may hear
the announcer say in his sonorous voice,
*Robert Spicer, seventy-two, of Osceola Mills,*
and remember the dusty horse barn, remember
the boy who showed you his penis, said
he'd measured it with his school ruler.
But you forget what the measurement was.

# Planning the Family Reunion

*for Barb*

While we sit, gently stirring
the air with your porch swing,
the green gauze of spring
    shimmers
           in the valley below.

As I fish the first gnat of the season
from my teacup, you tell me
    of a new shadow
          on your radiologist's screen.

When I loose your hand, you point
to the birdhouse where a pair of nuthatches
is hard at work enlarging the door—
    tap-tapping like tiny carpenters,
             she inside,
      he, out.

# Still Life, Kitchen Table

*for my father*

The clutter could be a portrait of him,
I think—but there's only this Steelers mug
stuffed with blunt pencils, pens long defunct.

And the matching glass shakers, one dusty
with pepper that's lost its pep. The other,
empty, I see.  Something to add to the list:

*Instant Oatmeal*
*Dinty Moore Stew*
*Salt*

On the far end, a welter of white envelopes,
bills mostly, along with an ad for Dish TV,
proclaiming superiority over cable.

There's a bag of bananas, going bad,
brown bowl with packs of crackers, 2-by-2,
to give body to a supper of canned soup.

And the magnifying glass without a handle—
a clear, round eye studying the ceiling,
the burned-out bulb.

# On the Morning of His Surgery, I Remember

Beside the stream, foaming and fussing
over the rocks in its bed, he hands me
a worm. It writhes and squirms,
shedding crumbs of dirt in my palm.

He's taught me how to do it—
how to pierce the red-brown skin
with the point of the hook, push
steady and slow, thread the worm

along the curve, bunch it up, leaving
an end free to wiggle in the current,
entice the trout that wears a rainbow
on its side. I don't remember

catching a fish. My worm, limp
and lifeless by now, was always nibbled
away by crayfish creeping pale and silent
along the bottom of the creek.

# Not Going to Buttonwood

The poem I'd planned to write left me
on Route 15. While I rhapsodized,
mentally, about the mountains—
how they folded like origami
around a lake with turquoise water—
my poem must have taken the exit
to Buttonwood.

I'd always wanted to see Buttonwood—
imagined a town with tiny brown houses
ranged in a row along a grosgrain road.
But this is no trip for sight-seeing.
I'm on a daughter-bound mission
to my father's bedside.

I catch sight of my poem
where the bypass meets Route 322,
but it's poking along below
the speed limit, so I toot, pull into
the passing lane, and wave sadly
as I hurry by.

In the hospital, asleep on his side,
my father is a collection of bones
and tubes and wires.  I sit down
in a green vinyl chair in the corner.
Nurses bustle by in the hall, footfalls
of sensible shoes brisk and familiar.

Then, the tentative step of a poem,
half-formed, and I look up to see it
standing in the doorway. I put my
finger to my lips, *Shhh*, and my poem
enters, chooses the chair at the foot
of the bed. Together, we watch
the rise and fall of my father's breath.

# Visiting Hours

*For my sister and my mother*

They cannot see what I see: sunlight falling through tall windows
to splash on a polished floor, wheelchairs placed here and there,

like metal sculptures—at once modern and medieval. And in these
chairs, seeming heaps of cloth, skeins of hair, bundles of bone.

Some sit alone, curled leaves burned by frost, waiting for the wind.
Others, like us, sit in clusters—complex family machines that mutter

and sigh, shifting loved ones to ease pain, disrupt the tyranny
of time.  But my mother and sister can't see these others, can't see

that others can see them, that my sister's nightdress has slipped
from her shoulder. There in her chrome wheelchair on the polished floor

my sister's breast is exposed—bare and beautiful like a Greek statue,
whole and perfect on her broken body. But she would want to be covered.

So I bend to her and murmur. I cup her warm breast in my hand,
lift the shoulder of her gown, place her breast under the soft blue cloth.

Her eyes search but cannot find me. Yet her smile, brighter than sunlight
streaming through tall windows, bathes the room, bathes me.

# April passes by

*It is spring and I am blind.*
*—Ruth Rendell*

I cannot see
the willow fronds
tender and green
draped over the air
like fringe.

Nor the shadow
of a mallard skimming
the grass as it flies
to meet its feathered self
at splashdown.

I cannot see
the lake breathing
softly before me,
its face spangled
with sun.

Yet I can hear
the church bells,
smell wind
in the weave
of your shirt.

# Still

When we noticed lunchtime voices
in the hall, the ding of a call button,
squeak of rubber soles on tile floors,

we knew the sound of her breathing
had ceased. For long moments,

her shoulder, under my hand,
remained warm. Then a stillness,
profound and deep, came upon her—

not of worldly sleep but
of rest unbounded by time.

All her ailments, her frailties,
fell away and the wholeness…
the holiness… which remained

gave her back to us
as she was, as she is.

# Because death has rendered you mute

I take the audacious step
to list for you
what you've left behind:

your blindness of course
the pain of arthritis
compression fractures of the spine

the ghost of poverty
tyranny of liquor
grief for a child lost

You've cast off your anger
justified though it was
left it in a heap next to the robe

with a broken zipper
and the slippers too tight
to fit your swollen feet

But you've taken with you
the laugh that filled your mouth
songs from the war years

answers to all the questions
in the Baltimore Catechism
mystery of midnight mass

You've taken your recipes for
penuche & homemade ice cream
how to can venison

the tale of Ninnykins & Tinnykins
your love of yellow leaves
and of sweet corn dripping butter

You've taken your half
of the memories

# Their Stone

Granite
   coarse and gray
except for the face
polished to a dark sheen
   and engraved
with the symbols he chose:

two birds
   gazing at each other
two rings
entwined on a vine
   embracing their names
the important dates

I think of the nature
   of tethers and chains
of her blindness
claiming his patience
   taming him
to her side

Each day
   for years
he spooned
mashed potatoes
   canned peas
into her waiting mouth

her need
   feeding his
to be needed

# Fount

Today at church we sang *Al-le-lu-ia, al-le-lu-ia*
and from my throat soared my mother's voice.

She was in the bellows of my lungs, the cave
of my skull, pouring from my mouth.

And shimmering there on the hymnal, an image
of her, head thrown back, eyes closed,

mouth a perfect oval, shaped by the vowels
as they now shaped mine. Down the years

flowed a river of songs, carried on chords
from organ, piano, guitar. Or simply sung

in the kitchen over the ironing board.
Now that she's gone, she is ever with me.

Each Sunday, I will be her voice—her sorrow
in the somber tones, in crescendo, her joy.

# The Clarity of Crossroads

# On Fitzgerald Road

Light, late-day, lies aslant
the stubbled fields, triangulates roads
laid out on a grid.  I am reassured

by this geometry, comforted by
right angles, the clarity of  crossroads—
their cruciformed arms stretching

horizon to horizon—and I think of
the blackberry thicket where
brambles grabbed my hair,

thorns brought beads of blood on
sun-scorched arms, midges danced,
black, before my eyes, and I believed

I would die there, entangled,
strung up and flailing,
like a doe in barbed wire.

# Raspberry House, 1968

*A big kitchen!* I crowed.
A wrap-around porch to hug the house.
Twenty-five acres, half of it woodlot.

   I forgot the rocks in the soil, swamp
   at the bottom of the slope.

After all, there were brown-eyed Susans
shouting by the hen house, a bow-window
to smile at visitors, if any were to come.

   In the bedroom, I closed my eyes
   to walls painted black.

When our boy dropped a marble
in the parlor, it rolled without pause
into the far corner. Yes, there were signs

but I missed them, taken as I was with
the raspberry canes beside the barn, bowed
to the ground with their delicate burden.

# Woodstoves 101

When did woodstoves become
romantic?  I'm guessing 1968
when the back-to-the-land movement
flourished like zucchini plants—
prolific, ubiquitous, self-important.

Our stove—black and unadorned—
smacked of practicality, squatting there
on the blue linoleum. Its pipe snaked
across the living room near the ceiling,
then burst out through the wall,

gasping, for it didn't always draw well.
On windy days, down drafts belched
smoke into the house and we ate
supper with streaming eyes
that had nothing to do with onions

I'd fried to flavor the venison.
It mingled with the smell of two
redbone hounds, wet and steaming,
perfumed our hair, our clothes,
marking us as novices from the city.

At Galusha's General Store, they looked
up, startled, when we walked in to buy
galoshes and bug spray, essentials for life
on our 25 acres—one-third swampland,
all of it clouded with blackflies.

# Flat Black

He'd painted the stove
in the parlor a dull black,
fitting somehow, for the task
of burning his mother's gift.

Twenty dollars, not much today,
but then, it was groceries
for a week, a trip to the vet
for our Redbone hound,

sick and shivering by the stove.
As the flame reached up
to taste the bill, it flared
around his fingers, singed

the fine hairs on his hand,
made it easy for him to let go,
close the lid and climb
the stairs to our bedroom

under the eaves. I waited
a long time after the floorboards
creaking above my head
went silent.

# Subsistence, 1968

Grace is a fool
for cinnamon rolls
She waits
drooling
by the fence
the snuffle
of her blunt snout
audible
long before
I get to the barn

Sometimes
she stands up
rests
her front trotters
delicately
on the rail
and smiles
when I come
through the door
bearing

stale sweets
from the thrift store
As she gobbles
the rolls
from the trough
I scratch her
bristled back
with a stick
She grunts
with pleasure

The man
who comes
for her
has a stick too
Grace chases him
into a corner
so he hits her snout
Blood drips onto
the clean straw
I look away

She comes back
to me
wrapped
in white paper
taped and
neatly labeled
I place her
one package
at a time
in the deep freeze

# Then ... and Then

You were with her, and I
with him. We sat at your table,
eyes on the string beans, the salad.
Four-part conversation played
against a background of rain
and roiling thunder.

I saw your fork poised
mid-air, your eyes fixed
on the white curtains
streaming out, not in,
the open window.

Then a sound like a cliff face
calving, a mountain split asunder,
and through the window
a ball of blue light
crackled and smoked,
an electric tumbleweed
rolling across the floor
and out the other window.

A piece of the heavens,
I thought; he thought
a piece of hell.
We were both right.
Our schism widened, our unit
cleaved by the ball of lightning,
leaving a smell of ozone,
a new fusing of the elements,
you and me.

# One

*For Federico Garcia Lorca*
*and for Andrew*

When the moon sails out,
the winds of wisdom at her back,
her face betrays nothing of the suffering
she's seen—of choices made
that were not choices, but aftermaths,
inevitable as the waters that covered
the earth after forty days of rain.

Two-by-two left some behind to tread
water. Yet, by grace, there was one
who could swim, whose heart
did not shrink, but grew stronger
with each stroke, who beat the sea
until his feet felt sand and he stood
erect, a little island in the infinite.

# Kitchen Therapy

Spare me the whine
of electric beaters
   blades that whirl
      pulverize    peel

hulking bread machines
   juicers   grinders
lurking like robots
on the countertop

I want to whip
thick cream
with a wire whisk
   knead yeasty dough
with bare hands

        feel it fight back

I want to scald tomatoes
in steam    slip them
from their tender skins
   expose flesh

       weeping red

Let me strip an onion
from its parchment
   chop   dice   mince
with my steel-bladed knife

Never mind the tears
   they don't need answers
      and no one asks

# Sometimes I Agree With Frost:
## *Nothing Gold Can Stay*

Please don't tell me the sun
will rise. I can't ignore the night
following behind—sightless beast
tethered by a chain of hours.

There are days I rejoice in the dawn,
celebrate the snowdrop, but sugar
dissolves quickly while bile lingers,
bitter in the back of the throat.

I don't want to hear about spring.
Every crocus, brave in the wind,
each leaf, tender and green, carries
the timetable for its own decay.

# In this poem

I want to say something to comfort you.
I want my words, like old shoes, to fit
without pinch or rub, drape over your shoulder
like a favorite sweater, simmer on the stove,
lifting a little cloud of steam to mist the face

of the kitchen clock tick-ticking each moment
into lemon drops. I'll find a word to billow
the curtain at the window, another to pour into
the room with sunlight, pool on the faded carpet
at your feet. If you want someone with you,

I'll choose a whisper-word—sister, maybe—
to sit at your side, click-clicking her needles
and yarn. If solitude is what you seek,
I promise you silence, and space for your heart
to float freely and for sleep, when it comes.

# No Opinions, No Needs

When you come out of the house,
a line of worry between your brows,

we sigh with you. It's a sigh that means
a breeze is passing, nothing more.

We are the leaves. We have no opinions,
no needs for you to fill. Maple, poplar, oak—

common as the common man, we wave
our multitudinous hands above you.

Even if you don't see us, still we wave.
Let us breathe with you, for you are one

of us. Let us dapple you with coolness,
drape our lacy shade over your shoulders.

Let us show you how to be, for we know
when to come, when to go.

# Wild Geese

it seems late
to undertake
such a journey
   but there they are
just days before
Christmas
   heading south

so high
their cries
are thready
   and faint

their V wavers
across
the slate sky—
   a scribble made
   by a careless hand

when they veer north
   I worry
then remember
the lake

and that life
is not meant
   to be lived
in a straight
line

# After Forty Years

In his office, I unfold my spreadsheet
before the parish priest.
He wants to smile, but does not.

I recite each trespass,
stain the pages with my tears,
and wait, expecting lectures,

Our Fathers and Hail Marys,
rosaries enough to reach
around the world.

If there were a clock
in the room,
it would be ticking.

The priest clears his throat
and in the voice he'll use later
to buy a roll at the bakery,

grants me absolution,
pronounces my penance—
*Perform two acts of kindness,* he says.

Can it be this simple?
The telling, the weeping,
the kindness?

# Yesterday's Snow, Tomorrow's Garden

# Cold Spring

*This is the season of not yet.*

Fr. Gurdon Brewster

That groan you hear
comes from the frozen throat
of the river where ice heaves,
makes ready to jostle and crash
its way downstream.

When the last floe rounds
the bend by the barn,
the river will run fast and free,
flirt with topping its banks.
But not yet.

Snow lies in patches on the grass
so you venture out without boots.
On the path through the trees,
you sink ankle-deep in slush,
soaking your socks.

Icicles drip in syncopation
from the branches above,
pock the snow, soft at your feet.
A chickadee brings his mate
a caterpillar still stiff with frost.

Yet already, skunk cabbage has shoved
bright tips above the snow.  Soon,
violets will wriggle through leaf mold.
Trillium and trout lilies, bluets and
bloodroot will follow.  You know

the day will come when you can walk,
dry-shod, to the spring in the woods,
bow down and drink from the chalice
of your hands, water tasting of
yesterday's snow, tomorrow's garden.
                    But not yet.

# Backyard Biologist

She sings out the identities
of wildflowers—birdsfoot trefoil,
butter and eggs, spotted knapweed,
Deptford pinks—as if introducing you
to particular friends of hers.

*Divers and dabblers*, she declares
of the ducks floating and bobbing
in the shallows. *Common Merganser,*
she crows, flipping through
Peterson's Guide to confirm.

Lying on her back among leaves
fallen from the poplars, the sugar maples,
the sweet gum, she sighs with satisfaction—
*Stratus, cirrus, cumulonimbus*—
enjoying the sibilance.

Of that birdsong floating flute-like
from the deciduous forest at dusk—
*Hermit Thrush! Or is it Veery?*
She's never sure, and this vexes her.
You want to ask, can't you be happy

with Bird? Leaf? Cloud? Flower?
You want to take her back to board books
and a bright yellow disk labeled SUN,
a brown stick holding up a green ball,
quite content to be just TREE.

# Intrepid

*for Kyle*

Once, I asked if you remembered
the day we braved the downpour.
How we bolted from the house, afraid
the rain would end too soon,

how the drops drummed our skulls,
dripped from our lashes, puddled
in the hollows of our collar bones,
the potholes on the road. You said

you didn't, smiled a bit sadly.
Of course, I thought, you were
only three.  So I tell you, here,
how the gutters gushed brown water,

how we gathered twigs and leaves,
squatted and launched our fragile
crafts on the river rushing
in the ditch. We laughed when they

capsized, cheered when they made it
past the manhole cover, clapped
when one of yours broke free
from a stick that blocked its way.

You pumped your little fist skyward,
grinning.

# Standing On the Footbridge Over Buttermilk Creek

in the still green pool
minnows school
then scatter
we give up counting
guess a hundred

the number
nudges memory
and the boy
recalls
show and tell

*bring one hundred*
*of something*
the teacher had said
thinking
pebbles pennies stamps

the boy brought
one hundred
salamanders
and spent recess
in the corner

had I been
that teacher
this boy would have
a hundred gold stars
on his forehead

next time
he'd bring
one hundred
comets
in his pocket

one hundred
clouds
on
a silver
string

# Geranium

I don't blame you. It's me has kept you
in that coffee mug. Gangly and gawky,
you must be strangling on your roots.

But you were a gift—Mother's Day
years and years ago—from a young son
with empty pockets, and my heart wants you

to stay where you were planted. You stand
on the sill above the sink, mere inches from
the faucet. Still I often fail to give you water

until I see one of your leaves has dropped,
dry and disconsolate. Yet this morning,
I came into the kitchen and there,

resting against the window like the head
of a weary traveler on a bus, was a bloom
so red, it sang.

*(for Ian, with thanks)*

# The Celestron

It lives in the basement between the water heater
and a bank of black metal shelves loaded with tools,
half-empty paint cans.  Shrouded in cobwebs,
it stands, dejected, staring at the concrete floor.

For a time I felt guilty for its plight. Now I no longer
see it when I go to retrieve a screwdriver, put towels
in the washer.  It's become part of the basement,
like the water heater, black shelves, paint cans.

Last night, the sound of steps on the basement stairs
startled me from sleep. Then came the rasp of the door
to the deck sliding in its track. I crept from my bed,
picked up the broom from the kitchen, just in case,

and stepped into the front room. There was no moon,
but starlight bathed the floor, the furniture, the deck
where the telescope stood, its three legs braced wide,
barrel pointed to a sky awash with silver.

*Come,* it whispered. *Come and see.*

# He Wrote Himself on the Sky

*for Philippe Petit*

defiant of laws
  even gravity's

defiant of a fear

so primitive
it stops
the breath

that small man
  poised
one foot
on the tower's edge

one
on the wire
  stretched
over nothing
except air
and taxi horns

there was a moment
  he said
when he shifted
his weight
from building
to wire

and all fear
left him

  what remained
was grace

# The Art of Walking

On the sculpture *Walking Man*
by Alberto Giacometti

*I am here*  I say
walking
    and here…
    and here…
myself in all places

each moment
pinches me
    into a new shape
    tests
the armature hidden within

but the mere act of being
upright
    a vertical stroke
    against the horizon
is enough

I carry me with me
a moving pillar
    between ground
    and sky
propelled by breath and longing

*Weatherside* by Andrew Wyeth

# Government Worker, 1966

I forget his name—the man in my office
at NSA. A quiet, colorless man who

shyly admired the green of my dress.
The next day he brought a book.

It needed two hands to hold and was
full of pages of Wyeth paintings—

*Grasses, old wood… How I loved*
*the dryness! All juices removed by sun,*
*wind, and time. Green gone peaceful.*
*No longer longing.*

That day, the colorless man saw my longing
and with one quick move, tore a page

from his costly book, placed it in my hand.
*Weatherside.* I rolled it loosely, took it home

to my little flat where red bricks held the wet
DC heat, where windows looked out on concrete.

*Frostbitten* by Andrew Wyeth

# Frostbitten

I can't say what caught my breath
when I turned the page. The window's grid,

cruciform against a pale sky, emerging
once more from the years?

Straggle of bare branches, winters alone
far from town, the sound of their scratching

on the pane? Maybe it was the sill, nicked
and peeling, the wall darkened by time

and smoke from a feeble fire long quenched.
But certainly it was the apples—four of them,

gnarled and mottled red—holding even now
the stubborn promise of a bit of sweetness.

*Evening Velvet* by Anita Dore

# Symbiosis

You there, in front of that painting—
following the curve of the hill
with your eyes, letting them linger
on the pond, feeling now
the breeze that ruffled the water
into tiny wavelets—

do you know that the peace
stealing over you
is the same the artist knew
when her brush laid down
that particular shade
of blue?

And when you read a poem,
feel the shape of each word
in your mouth, hear it ring
like a vesper bell, do you understand
that without you the words are stones
at the bottom of a well?

When an acorn sprouts among leaf mold,
when the phoebes fledge, launching
one by one into air soft with spring,
when the newborn knows how to nurse
at his mother's breast, do you see
that you, too, are called?

# The Oldest People at the Party

I see you across the kitchen, laughing
with a young father who might have been
you, forty years ago, a toddler hugging

your bell-bottomed leg. *My* youthful
counterpart cradles an infant at her breast,
talks of her organic peas, homemade salsa,

handmade clothes. I want to give her
my old recipe for Consciousness III,
with carob. Children with daddy-barbered

hair swirl among us like brilliant leaves.
Folk music mingles with many voices, swells
with my heart, for I am loving these young families.

I am loving *us,* as we were then
when we, too, invented
the world.

# I Want to Say the Stars Were Like Diamonds on Black Velvet

I want to say that when we, more than 40 years a couple,
closed the door on the party, muffled the swirl of young voices,
skirl of bright music, and stepped out, just we two, into
November night, we cued the next stage of our lives.

I want to say that when you tucked my hand into the curve
of your arm, and we walked, blinded by darkness, down
the rutted road, past the moonless barking of dogs,
it depicted our past, foreshadowed our future.

I want to say that when we climbed the hill to the top and stopped—
breath ragged, legs aching—the stars were like diamonds
on black velvet, silver minnows caught in the net of bare branches,
heaven shining through pinpricks in the fabric of sky.

# From the cradle

I have been blessed
by the best of them—
old bishops in mitered hats
cardinals in namesake red.

From their elevated stations
one step closer to God, they reach
into a storehouse of faith,
their reservoir of wisdom,

and confer a bit of it
on me. I am the receiver.
I try to open my heart,
envision a flower

in the rain, and am,
sometimes, nourished.
But yesterday,
in a moment alone with him,

I placed a palm on my infant
grandson's brow, thinking,
in my poor way, to bless.
In an instant I knew

the sacred was already there.
Goodness newly-minted,
innocent as first light,
        he blessed me.

# Prayer for Wendy

One of many, of course, but this prayer
is so small—and so large—that I must
tell you now, while the leaves blaze
against  a sky so gray and soft it would
feel like flannel if you could but touch it.

> Life is October for me.  Nearness
> to the end of the year heightens its joy,
> deepens its sorrow.  And I celebrate
> and grieve every leaf.

> Do you know there's a tiny sound
> when a leaf lets go its twig?  That it
> whispers down the air?  Sighs when
> it comes to rest?

Of course you do.  And that's my prayer
for you, dear girl. That you stay mindful,
as you are now. That when you are sewing
you will always love the sound the thread
makes when it glides through the cloth.

# Isabel

The mug
   chunky and white
says on its side
   *I love my grandma*

A sprinkle
   of tiny hearts
circles
   the words

I sip
   milky tea
my glasses
   cloud with steam

Outside
   snow so weightless
it isn't even falling
   floats

in front
   of the window
If I hold
   my breath

maybe
   time will stop
my tea
   will never cool

the little girl
   who wrapped
this mug
   in bright paper

will stay
   eight years old
With my eyes
   I choose

a single flake
   from
the thousands
   filling the air

follow its flight
   as it dances
this way
   and that

until
   it touches
the pane
   lingers

then melts
   becoming again
a drop
   of clear water

# At Three ...

If we can know the ocean
in a drop of water
    the earth
        in a grain of sand
then too we can hear
    every woe of the world
in the cry of one little boy

It started small
    something he longed for
        lost
but grew
    gathering grief down the ages
until it consumed him
    overwhelmed all sound
        voices
        music from the radio
        motor of the car
in which he rode     strapped
into his seat
        confined    comfortless

His wail came
From deep in his body
    wracking the tiny frame
with sobs
    desolate as a city of ashes
    funeral rain
            on a black umbrella

# On the floe

Water gray and ice-flecked
surges in the ever-widening gap
between where we stand and
the land where sons work
love their wives tend babies
wash cars mow lawns
have beers with their friends
sing songs we don't know
tell stories of growing up
which if we heard them
would be about strangers
we wouldn't recognize
as ourselves
the fools the saints the villains
who walk through these tales
coming in one side going out
the other like figures on a roll
of paper in a shoebox diorama

# Now, in the evening

You sit
in the wingchair
open your sewing box
and lamp light
flows in

How fragile and brave
the spools of thread
ranged in rows
of red and blue
violet and green

Needle in hand
do you remember
knees worn through
seams undone
rends long and jagged

Do you recall
countless patches
careful stitches
safety pins when
time was short

This evening
will you lay aside
the shirt
with frayed cuff
coat with no buttons

Will you choose
a square of fair linen
embroider
on its corner
a small yellow rose

# Winter Trees Have No Secrets

# The Seasons of Trees

The trees are putting on their clothes
again, assuming the softer, rounder shapes
of summer. Soon, they'll sway

with a grace impossible in winter,
stand at the edge of the stream
trailing fringe in the current,

wait in ranks along the road, wave
multitudinous hands at each passing car,
drape shadow lace over old men sleeping.

But I miss their bones—bare and brave
in the wind, calligraphic against the sky,
for winter trees have no secrets—

each scar speaks of injury endured,
a wound healed. That jagged slash remembers
lightning, those severed twigs, a hungry deer.

Winter trees make no complaint—
simply shrug the snow from naked limbs,
stir the stars with patient fingers.

# Currency

Time has his hand in my pocket
but I never feel his bony fingers.
I know I've been robbed only
when I try to spend the coins
I thought were still there.

I know only when my aching knee
keeps me from climbing
to the top of the hill.
When no one in my office
has heard Jack Benny's jokes
or the clink of glass milk bottles
on the porch at dawn.
When the handsome young man
passes me on the street and his eyes show
not the faintest flicker.

I am becoming invisible.
I am almost bankrupt.
Youth is the coin of the realm
and my pocket is nearly empty.

Some would say that Time is trading
wisdom for youth.
But wisdom is foreign currency
from a failing nation.
When I take it from my pocket,
press the wrinkles flat,
only my friends will accept it.
On the open market
it buys nothing.

# On this birthday

Seven and Zero stand back-to-back.
Seven wears a jaunty cap,
a snap-brimmed affair
in a tasteful tweedy plaid.

Zero is plump and innocently naked,
her cheeks untouched by blush,
because, luckily, Seven is turned away
looking to the past.

Slightly sway-backed, he surveys it all,
placidly at first, then draws himself up
in alarm as he sees pages fly,
day-by-day, off the calendar—

twenty-five thousand,
five hundred sixty-eight
of them swirling down the black
and white streets of a 1940s movie.

Zero rocks on her bottom,
weeble-like. Should she stay put,
settle for the status quo?
Or can she muster from somewhere

deep in her soft middle
a burst of energy that will send her
tumbling, headlong and hopeful,
into her foreshortened future?

## Love in the latter days

I fall in love easily
and often
these days
   on monday
a common redpoll
pecking seeds on the deck
with his pencil-point beak
   stirred my heart

on tuesday
it was a fox
   coat flushed
   with sunset
   tiny black boots barely
touching the grass
as she trotted
to the hedgerow

later when I looked
into the woods
through the window
above the sink
   a fallen log
   cushioned in moss
   the color of Ireland
stopped my breath

and just now
there above the trees
a vulture
   flawless
   and purposed
rocks in the sky
fingered wings
spread wide

# Lucy at the Book Group

A few days ago when I started this poem
I made the mistake of telling someone
about Lucy the Dog, who was its subject.
I described her—medium-sized, black,

except for the gray, like hoar frost, around
her eyes, her muzzle, as if she'd been snuffling
the grass on a crisp morning. So as every poet
knows, when you talk about your poem,

it leaves you, and Lucy faded until only
her eyes were left, brown and still as a cup
of well-steeped tea, gazing at me, asking
for nothing. But now, as I write again,

I can see the way she held her head when
she visited my knees, leaning into my hand
as I cupped the perfect shape of her skull.
And I remember now that when the meeting

started Lucy went to the center of the circle,
settled herself with a sigh, and lay on her side,
four legs pointing right.  Soon, a gentle snore
like the smolder of the small fire on the hearth.

We people—five of us—seated on sofas
and chairs, talked in lofty words about God
and acceptance—his of us, ours of him—
and I found myself yearning toward Lucy.

I longed to lie down beside her, lay my arm
over her body, rising, falling in a timeless
rhythm, and put my nose to hers—
two old girls, breathing together.

# Mind Matters

The secret latch is hidden behind
my left ear. If you press it, the door
of my forehead will swing open
and you can see the stuff with angel
names: Cerebrum, Cerebellum—
rows and rows of cubbyholes
like the ones in an old roll-top desk.

See, there in a box called BASICS—
the alphabet. (In block letters and
in script.) And the multiplication
tables, a bit dusty now that we have
pocket calculators. There's no slot for
Foreign Languages, except for the one
marked IG-PAY ATIN-LAY.

The largest compartment is labeled
MISCELLANEOUS. It holds things
like touch-typing, a recipe for molasses
cookies, the Library of Congress
classification system, how to thread
a Singer sewing machine, and the name
of the redbone hound I had in Maine.

That cubbyhole in the very center?
I've cleared it to make more room
for MYSTERY. (Some might call it
my God niche.)  Right now it holds
only a nautilus shell, an acorn, and
a scrap of paper with the 23rd Psalm.
But I'm still searching.

# Utah, off State Route 24

In the green world, what passes for silence
is, in truth, a quiet cacophony
of rustles, murmurs, whispers, sighs.

But here, there are no leaves
to be stroked by wind fingers,
stirred by bird wing, only

stark red canyons, blue vitrified sky.
And silence is, in truth, heart-thud,
blood-surge, rib-creak.

I burn to sit here, bareheaded
under the fierce eye of the sun
until I hear that still, small voice.

After forty days, forty nights,
surely I'll hear it. Surely I, too,
will inhabit the edge

where John the Baptist reeled
in divine madness,
eating locusts and wild honey.

# Looking Out

this rain
these willows
yellow fronds
draped
like fringe
over the pond

these ducks
dabblers all
comical tails
turned up
nibbling bills
sieving for food

this hand
holding bread
tipping
the cup
to sip
to swallow

this pain
in my side
familiar foe
familiar friend
forever
reminding me

I am less
than spirit
and more

# Murmuration

Have you ever seen it?
A vast cloud of birds
casting itself in broad sweeps
across the sky?

And have you heard
the rush of wings
as all those birds dip and soar,
fold and fling as one?

&

I think of Simon, called Peter,
and Andrew his brother,
their arms strong
and bronzed by the sun,

spreading their nets in the Sea
of Galilee, a heartbeat before
they are called to follow
and become fishers of men.

&

Once, in a rarified moment,
I knew myself to be
a murmuration,
composed of multitudes,

yet at the same time,
a single, dark,
iridescent starling,
identical to all the others.

# Where, then?

With dread, I look toward the day I can
no longer drive. Oh, I know someone
can take me to the store. And Gadabout
will come to my door and deliver me
to my doctor or dentist.  But no more

nosing my car into a worn track in the woods
where, safe from rain, I can study brambles
and branches, tease words from the tangle
and scratch them onto a pad of paper
resting on the steering wheel.

No longer will I park near hydrangea bushes
at the cemetery and read Flannery O'Connor's
*Prayer Journal*, lift my eyes from time to time
and gaze at gravestones, stealing their silence
as the backdrop for my own prayer.

Never again will I sit alone at the harbor
where gulls carry light on their backs.
And boats resting at anchor sway their masts
like metronomes, ticking away the moments
of solitude into which God speaks.

# Churchyard

On this November day
with hills and fields
a hundred shades of brown
sky a hundred shades of gray
this cemetery seems the right place to be

But I'm not thinking of the present dead
lying in their brown beds
with headboards of marble
and granite
slicked by the rain

Nor of the nearly dead
waiting on the threshold
in field hospitals
emergency rooms
nursing homes

Or the oblivious young
their speakers thumping
in low-slung cars
slewing now
around a curve

Most of all
I'm not thinking of myself
my accumulated years
weary bones and spirit
palpitating heart

I'm thinking of that little sparrow
over there
scuffing in the damp leaves
his black cravat and gray cap
bright searching eye

# Three Ways to Go

*A photography professor at the University of Florida
just happened to see a bird die, mid-flight.*
Annie Dillard, *Pilgrim at Tinker Creek*

Robert died with his arms in the air,
baton poised to cue the percussion. The band
was barely four bars from the beginning, but
Robert's heart was already at the final beat.

He teetered on the proscenium for the space
of a grace note, then tumbled backwards
off the stage into the arms of the audience,
suit coat billowing as he fell.

\* \* \*

Rosalie spent her last breath in a laugh,
the story she'd told still hovering above
the table.  Her husband—the third and
very best—turned to grin at her across

empty cups and crumpled napkins.
He wondered at her closed eyes, touched
with trepidation her hand, now cooling.  Oh,
did I mention Rosalie had finished dessert?

Had allowed the last bite of coconut cream pie
to dissolve sweetly in her mouth. Retrieved
an errant crumb and placed it on her tongue.
Laid her fork neatly on the clean china plate.

\* \* \*

As for me, perhaps I'll die sweeping.
My broom will move across the kitchen floor,
chasing the soft snips of your hair, silver now
after all these years of wifely haircuts.

I'll have brushed them from your shoulders,
dropped a kiss on your balding crown.
I'll hear you calling from the shower
as I let go the broom, sink slowly down,

You'll be saying something about mowing
the lawn. Or you'll ask if I'd like to go
to McClary's for an ice cream after dinner.
I'll want, very much, to say yes.

# Exit Strategies

A linen sheet would be nice.
White, of course, and not wound
too tightly. I'll want to have my hands
free to scratch my nose when
those tiny rootlet hairs in the fresh
grave tickle it.

I'll pass on a casket, thank you.
Even the thought of an MRI makes me
hyperventilate, so I can't imagine
what the cover of a coffin would do,
creaking closed. I don't care how much
white satin lines the lid!

But cremation might be a good choice,
if I may romanticize it a bit. Perhaps
it would be like merging with the sun—
white-hot, clean. And it's rather appealing
to think of my plump self made compact
enough to fit into an urn.

I've saved the best option for last, though.
Now please don't think me pompous
or proud, but wouldn't it be a blast
to be sent off as fireworks?! First, a boom,
which the watcher would feel, deep
and profound, in the bass drum of the chest.

Then a burst of color—red, blue, gold
and silver stars streaking into the sky,
blazing themselves on blackness.
A comet, a super-nova in miniature,
the last chance for an ordinary woman
to shine before her ashes drift down

and settle on the trampled grass
of the high school football field
where, once, she cartwheeled
under stadium lights, cheering
loudly for the team that in 1960
went undefeated.

# Tundra

If I go on I fear I'll find
only cold.  Blinded by light
unseen I turn round and round,
seeking the last cairn—
    the one I made
    moments ago.
Or yesterday.

I think to go back
to that place where stones
held the warmth of the sun,
where small flowers
    sheltered
    by what we'd built
blossomed.

But the tower of rock is gone,
long since fallen away,
so I go on.
The vastness
    opens its arms
    and the horizon
beckons at the edge.

# Break Me Open

This body is a box
locked by life
    corporeal casket for
    a soul grown stale

My third eye's nearly blind
yet still it scans
the long road worn to ruts
    brown bird singing
    the same brown song

Break me open
let me rise
    like steam from
    this stew of myself

Let me mingle
with clouds until
I fall as rain
    on lilacs
    on cornfields

until I reach
    the fathomless sea

The title poem, "Planting Wild Grapes," follows as a Coda.

This version, however, concludes with a 4th stanza that mirrors an important yet enigmatic thought and gift of the spirit:

*Everything matters. And nothing matters.*

# Planting Wild Grapes

Every day at dawn I go down to the river,
fill my bucket to the brim and wash stones.
Big or small, I take all that come to hand,
dip them in my pail, rub them between my palms
and drop them back into the river. I listen
for the satisfying sound—the watery thunk—
as they settle among their fellows.

At mid-day I wade the waves of goldenrod
to the center of the sunny field behind the barn.
Beneath my feet my shadow crouches,
small and black. The candle in my hand
stands tall, like me, its wick waiting for
the match, prepared to be proud of a flame
invisible in the noonday light.

Sunset finds me again at river's edge, a teacup
cradled in my hands. It holds rainwater caught
in the downpour at dinnertime. I lift it up
to the sinking sun, see the rim turn gold,
then tip the cup, spilling rain into the river.
Tomorrow, if I keep to my course,
there will be time to plant wild grapes.

And if tomorrow doesn't find me, the river
will run, bathe each stone in its bed.
The sun, at its pinnacle, will blanch wheat
and weeds to near-white. Rain will dimple
the river's skin, wild grapes will self-seed,
taking root in black soil. And my children
will breathe on without my breath,
but with my prayers.